TONY SHAFRAZI EDITIONS

Patrick Demarchelier

Exposing Elegance

Text
Martin Harrison

Cover: Amber Valletta, 1997
ISBN: 1-891475-11-8
Design: Martin Harrison

2nd Revised Edition

119 Wooster Street New York, NY 10012
Tel 212 274 9300 Fax 212 334 9499

Patrick Demarchelier: Exposing Elegance was originally published in a bilingual Spanish-English edition to accompany the exhibition *Patrick Demarchelier: revelando la elegancia* organized by the Museo de Arte Contemporáneo de Monterrey, MARCO, and presented in Monterrey, Nuevo León, México from December 1997 to March 1998.

Tony Shafrazi Editions wishes to express its most sincere appreciation to Patrick Demarchelier, to the curator of the exhibition at MARCO and author Martin Harrison, and to Xavier López de Arriaga and the Museo de Arte Contemporáneo de Monterrey MARCO for their invaluable collaboration.

We would also like to acknowledge the following individuals:

Amanda Harrison
Ben Harrison
Ramiro Martínez
Wendell Maruyama
Hiroko Onoda
Jeffery Pavelka

Patrick Demarchelier: Exposing Elegance was originally published in a bilingual Spanish-English edition to accompany the exhibition *Patrick Demarchelier: revelando la elegancia* organized by the Museo de Arte Contemporáneo de Monterrey, MARCO, and presented in Monterrey, Nuevo León, México from December 1997 to March 1998.

Contents

Patrick Demarchelier

Exposing Elegance

Martin Harrison

Patrick Demarchelier's career in photography–he began in 1963–has spanned more than three decades, a period that has witnessed major shifts in the ways that the photographic image is looked at and understood. To a certain extent his evolution as a photographer may be considered a paradigm for many of those changes.

Today, when an art museum mounts a major exhibition of photographs–many of them originally made for "commercial" purposes–we are inevitably reminded that only twenty years ago such an event would have been unheard of. In the United States of America, though to a lesser extent elsewhere, museums had established a tradition of displaying "art" photographs, but even in that country a one-person show that included fashion photographs was unknown in 1977. Since that time, the debates surrounding contemporary photography have shifted away from the orthodoxies and conservatism of the so-called purists of the medium. The notion that photographic excellence was inextricably linked to exquisite craftsmanship has been radically overturned, in favor of a pluralistic approach to analyzing the cultural significance and meaning of photographs. Patrick Demarchelier is, it so happens, a consummate craftsman whose skills, however, never obtrude; his is an intuitive rather than an intellectual talent, and he has drawn inspiration widely and intelligently from the history of his chosen medium.

Photography in the twentieth century has followed many different paths. By the 1920s it was being appropriated as a vital tool in the service of advertising and mass consumption, and gradually supplanted the work of artists and illustrators in that field. Its principal attribute, apart from the rapidity of the process, was its veracity–the photograph helped to confer at least a degree of truthfulness on even the most improbable claims of advertisers. Ironically, at the same time in Germany, the phenomenon of the photojournalist was born, whose imprimatur was, likewise, that the camera could record and reveal the truth about contemporary events. The newly available "miniature" lightweight 35mm cameras were conceived to use the same film stock as movie cameras, and their very portability gave rise to a kind of image that was hitherto unavailable, sharing the immediacy and potency of film newsreels. It will be evident that Demarchelier's photography deftly bridges these alternative traditions.

If these two applications–advertising and reporting–were at opposite poles, there were two other principal directions in photography during the first half of the century that fitted into neither category; that is, they were not "applied" photography in the service of something else. The first was photography as utilized or modified by artists–by the surrealists, constructivists, or collagists. The second (its seeds were sown in the nineteenth century by photographers from the various pictorialist groupings who sought parity with artists) was the purist school that grew out of the Photo-Secession. Photographers such as Paul Strand,

Alfred Stieglitz and Edward Weston insisted, like the Photo-Secessionists, on their status as artists. But they rejected the Secessionists' attempts to mimic the effects of painting (by graphic manipulation of the print surface) in favor of mastering techniques inherent in the photographic process.

This is necessarily an over-simplified version of the complexities of photographic history, but may serve as a description of its status quo until about 1950. By mid-century, however, certain photographers had risen to prominence, for example, Henri Cartier-Bresson, Brassaï, André Kertész and Bill Brandt–whose work might fit equally well into at least two of the above categories. The emergence of influential figures suchs as Robert Frank and William Klein in the 1950s rendered the former tidy classifications difficult to uphold, if not redundant. But while photography started to be acknowledged as a subject with inherent virtues, applied photography was still rigidly excluded from serious attention. The true situation was more complicated than the convenient sub-divisions suggested. Though the photography for Frank's seminal book *Les Américains* from 1958 was financed by Guggenheim grants, on emigrating to America in 1947 he had supported himself by working for magazines like *Harper's Bazaar*. Similarly, Klein's first publication, *New York* from 1956, was financed by the income earned from fashion photographs he made for *Vogue*.

This is not to suggest that anything would be gained from raising these photographers' commercial efforts to the level of their other work, but the fact that individuals like Robert Frank and William Klein had a foot in both camps, so to speak, was a factor in what has gradually occurred in photography in the latter part of this century, namely a blurring of the boundaries between commercial and "non-commercial" photography. For the art director of

Vogue in the 1950s, a principal reason for hiring William Klein, and later Bruce Davidson, was that their style of photography might be appropriated to infuse energy, "realism," and contemporaneity into the magazine. One result of these associations was a gradual breakdown of the prejudice against fashion photography. It was, therefore, in a slightly more propitious critical climate that a younger generation of photographers, including Patrick Demarchelier, embarked on their careers in the 1960s, nimbly crossing between former polarities.

When Demarchelier began as a fashion photographer, however, there was no reason to entertain the idea that his work could ever find its way onto the walls of a gallery or museum. Even when, by the 1980s, conditions had changed sufficiently to make this feasible, he was, for his own reasons, reluctant to exhibit his work in a context very different than that for which it was originally intended. It was not until 1995 that he was finally persuaded by Tony Shafrazi to consider an exhibition at his prestigious New York art gallery. By this time Demarchelier had become recognized as more than a fashion photographer; he had fully earned his reputation as a sensitive and distinguished portraitist, and had demonstrated that he was equally adept at photographing landscapes, animals and anthropological subjects. But it was as a fashion photographer that he had first emerged on the international scene.

The origins of professional fashion photography can be traced back into the nineteenth century, but effectively its inception occurred in 1914, when Baron de Meyer was put under contract by *Vogue*. While his credentials as a European aristocrat have never been confirmed, de Meyer had succeeded in attaining a position in society that was doubtless as attractive to *Vogue* as his considerable abilities as a photographer. When he was lured away by arch-rival

Harper's Bazaar in 1922 (a move followed by many others and prescient of Demarchelier's own change of editorial outlet in 1991), he was replaced at *Vogue* by Edward Steichen. Two leading Photo-Secessionists had, therefore, been co-opted into premier positions within fashion photography; Steichen, in particular, transcended his earlier misty romanticism and gradually brought a less rarified, more natural and hard-edged clarity to the genre. In 1933 the Hungarian news and sports photographer Martin Munkacsi, on a working visit to the United States of America, was persuaded to photograph beachwear for *Harper's Bazaar.* He approached the job as he would have a sports photograph, instructing the model to run before his camera. This was not the first non-static fashion photograph, and the story has assumed almost mythical status in the retelling, but Munkacsi's "action" approach proved popular and helped to firmly established an alternative idiom.

Thereafter, fashion photography continued to develop along lines of oscillating between the formal and the informal, between the carefully posed static image and one which conveyed the impression of movement, and from the studio tableau to the outdoor location. Demarchelier's photographs have tended, from the beginning, to be fluid, informal, and outdoors–though he is equally adept at creating informality in the studio where, for practical reasons, fashion photography often has to be done. One suspects, though, that he would resent being categorized as merely a capturer of movement, since in fact his range is extremely wide. The pragmatism that defines his approach is, no doubt, partly grounded in his photographic training; initially, his way of solving problems was learned from the base upwards, as it were, operating as a darkroom craftsman.

Born near Paris in 1943, Patrick Demarchelier grew up in the northern French port and industrial town of Le Havre. (It has been remarked that his fondness for beach locations and the sunny, airiness of many of his photographs more obviously suggests a childhood in Provence. But it should be remembered that the proto-impressionist painter Eugène Boudin, to whose work Demarchelier's is remarkably close in spirit, was born just along the Seine estuary from Le Havre, at Honfleur, and found his inspiration in the clear light of the local seascape. Echoes of Boudin's desire to "convey...this vastness, this delicacy, the brilliant light which transforms everything to my eyes" are frequently found in Demarchelier's photographs. Interestingly, an element of Boudin's paintings that was criticized by his contemporaries was inclusion of fashionably dressed holiday-makers.) Today, whether he is photographing in Mexico, Miami, or the West Indies, the specifics of the exact geographical location tend to be secondary to the atmosphere created by light and air. Never academically inclined, and unsure what to do with his life, Demarchelier was given his first camera for his seventeen birthday, and knew at once what his career must be.

His first full-time photographic job was in a small laboratory in northern France, printing and retouching passport pictures. At the age of twenty he moved to Paris, first working in another laboratory, printing news photographs. Next, he graduated from the darkroom to a position as assistant to a photographer who specialized in taking the covers of movie magazines. Six months later he became house photographer to the Paris Planning model agency, taking test photographs of their young models; his broad photographic education was finally heading in the direction he had sought, and the experience in posing ingénues at this stage of his career must have been invaluable. After a year he took another assistant post, this time with a leading photographer, Hans Feurer. Feurer was an art director-turned-

photographer who had perfected a graphically economical kind of fashion photograph which, tightly cropped to focus directly on the woman, achieved considerable impact on the magazine page. When Demarchelier joined him, Feurer had begun to work for the innovative English magazine, *Nova,* and was just about to take his first photographs, in 1968, for *Vogue.* He learned rapidly from this experienced professional and was soon in a position to strike out on his own. With commissions from *Elle* and *Marie-Claire,* among other magazines, it was not long before Demarchelier was established as a photographer in his own right.

He was in the right place at the right time. Paris, at the close of the 1960s, was regaining its position as the world center of fashion photography. Helmut Newton and Guy Bourdin were moving into the most original phases of their careers, vying with one another to see who could edge closer to the boundaries of what was morally acceptable as an image in *Vogue.* A loosely-knit group of younger photographers, known variously as the "Paris Mob" or the "Paris Mafia," included, besides Demarchelier, François Lamy, Uli Rose, Arthur Elgort, Alex Chatelain, and Mike Reinhardt. They reacted against the decadence or self-conscious seriousness of their contemporaries in favor of fashion photographs which were upbeat, informal, and with the spontaneity of a snapshot.

Demarchelier's breezy, light-hearted action photographs perfectly caught the mood of the time, ushered in the next phase of fashion photography, and ensured that he became one of the great success stories of Paris. They were noticed by Alexander Liberman, creative director of *Vogue,* who felt that the "casual" quality of this kind of photograph gave them human warmth; it made them accessible to their target audience, and reflected what he described as "the sense of purpose in a modern woman's life." By 1974 Demarchelier was

working for the American edition of *Vogue*, and in the following year he decided to emigrate and live in New York. He regularly returned to photograph in Paris, and in fact did not become a regular contributor to *Vogue* until 1979. Two years later he turned down a lucrative advertising commission in favor of working with one of the most influential fashion editors of recent times, Grace Coddington of British *Vogue*. He has cited this incident as "vital to the progress of his career," and it clearly marked a turning point in his creative development. He arrived at what might be termed his "mature style," though it is important to note that this is an ongoing process. His early darkroom training bore fruit in the impeccable quality of Demarchelier's black and white prints, and in his wonderfully limpid color; to these he has added an even greater elegance (at a time when this was in short supply in fashion photography), though none of these qualities have been attained at the expense of the graphic energy and engaging informality of his images.

Demarchelier's fashion photographs are frequently admired, in the fashion business, for their realism, though he is fully aware that fashion photographs are not intended to deal with the real world. But in a world founded on artifice he manages to make images that are unforced and convincingly spontaneous. As he himself simply puts it: "I like real laughter in my pictures." He avoids the temptation to overrationalize his photographs, as if to do so might remove, for him, an essential element of mystery. Alexander Liberman described him as "a gentle pioneer," sensitive "to the natural attractiveness of women," and the writer Glenn O'Brien characterized him as a worshipper of beauty. But if his reputation was founded on his fashion photographs–of women–he has ultimately become equally sought after for his portraits of celebrities.

960080-665-9

The first distinction one notices in evaluating Demarchelier's portraits is that, almost without exception, they are made in black and white. With the majority of the most successful fashion photographers (Irving Penn and Richard Avedon come to mind), one senses that they feel making a portrait to be a greater challenge, and possibly of more enduring importance. Demarchelier is no exception, and like his predecessors reserves black and white for the more serious matters. It has often been suggested that in portraiture an artist only has the head and hands to work with; it is a distinguishing feature of many of Demarchelier's portraits that he focuses on the head and crops tightly around the shoulder line, bringing the gesturing hands into the frame as an expressive element which he uses to great effect. It is a device he uses not only in his photographs of men (for example, Elton John, Tom Cruise, Christian Slater, Robert De Niro, Robin Williams) but also women (Jessica Lange, Princess Diana, Andie McDowell, Brooke Shields) and even (much more unexpectedly and of course minus the hands) when photographing a lion or a camel–animal portraiture (or anthro-pomorhism?). On other occasions he moves to almost the opposite extreme and pulls back his camera to a "long shot" position, in order to include an aspect of the sitter's environment so as to augment the description of their character (Hillary Clinton, Billy Joel, Julian Schnabel).

While Demarchelier is clearly interested in the human face in general (and as the scope of his portrait subjects testifies), it will have been noted that all of the individuals listed above are international celebrities. That he has become so much in demand as a photographer of media stars is no surprise. Even the most outwardly assured actor or actress is liable to become nervous or self-conscious in a portrait sitting, when so much of the image they seek

to project can depend on the results of a relatively brief interaction. It is in this kind of situation that Demarchelier's character becomes a key factor, since his charm and naturally relaxed personality evidently break down his sitters' inhibitions and encourage them to place their trust in him. That he is more interested in their characters than imposing his own ambitions or preconceptions on his subjects is clear from the results, which share a mood of open informality and are honest without being judgmental.

Among the most intriguing of the more recent developments in Demarchelier's work are his landscapes and photographs of wild animals. Whether the subject be giraffes or zebras in Tanzania, Egyptian pyramids or a nearly abstract wall in Saint Barthélemy, these photographs are characterized by Demarchelier's ability to handle space, which consistently imparts upon them a compelling, airy, openness. Closely related to these are his ethnographic studies, from Masai warriors to sumo wrestlers, a Tibetan priest or a Peruvian woman and child. While these subjects partly reflect the extensive amount of travelling that he does, there is often little to separate them in intention from his photographs of models. He is clearly interested in the personalities of his female models, and some of his photographs of them have more in common with portraits than with fashion photographs, for example, those of Kristen McMenamy, Linda Evangelista, and Christy Turlington. In fact, Demarchelier can claim to have played an important part in the rise to star status of many of the "supermodels" of today. The position they now enjoy as international media personalities is due in no small part to his sympathetic portrayals of their characters. His fascination with the unclothed body is one shared by many fashion photographers; his professional interest in the way a woman's body moves when inside a garment seems to extend quite logically into a study of

the naked female form, and has been responsible for some of his most highly regarded images.

Finally, special mention deserves to be made concerning Demarchelier's use of color. Color photographs began to predominate in fashion magazines in the 1970s, and it has long been imperative that Demarchelier produce high quality transparencies for reproduction. Starting in the mid-1980s, however, he began, whenever the opportunity arose, to reclaim control over the range of colors in his photographs; among outstanding early examples of this development may be cited his photographs of dancers, *Mud Woman, Woman on the Beach,* and *Talisa Soto.* Too few commercial photographers appear to give sufficient consideration to the special requirements of structuring planes of colors, and the result is usually arbitrary or strident and inharmonious. Demarchelier, on the other hand, limits his palette to great effect; so, for example, by selecting a background color close to that of the dresses, he transforms graphically quite simple compositions, such as those of Mathilde, into images of considerable subtlety. His photograph of Kristina allies the same refined color sensibility to a striking and unusual pose; another photograph of the same model in a yellow coat is an example of a color harmony successfully obtained in the even more problematical circumstances of photographing on location.

One of the most recent developments in Demarchelier's work provides an exception to the norm mentioned earlier, in that he has made portraits of *The Artist Formerly Known As Prince* from 1997 in color as well as in black and white. Dramatic color prints from this session suggests a potentially exciting new direction for Demarchelier, just as his *Spring 1997 Paris Collections* series and the photograph of Amber Valletta confirm his continuing evolution as a colorist, and his position as one of the master photographers of today.

كازينو فلسطين
مشروبات
ماكولات
DRINKS
FOOD
PALESTINE CLUB
كوكا كولا
سبرايت

R.Nº4

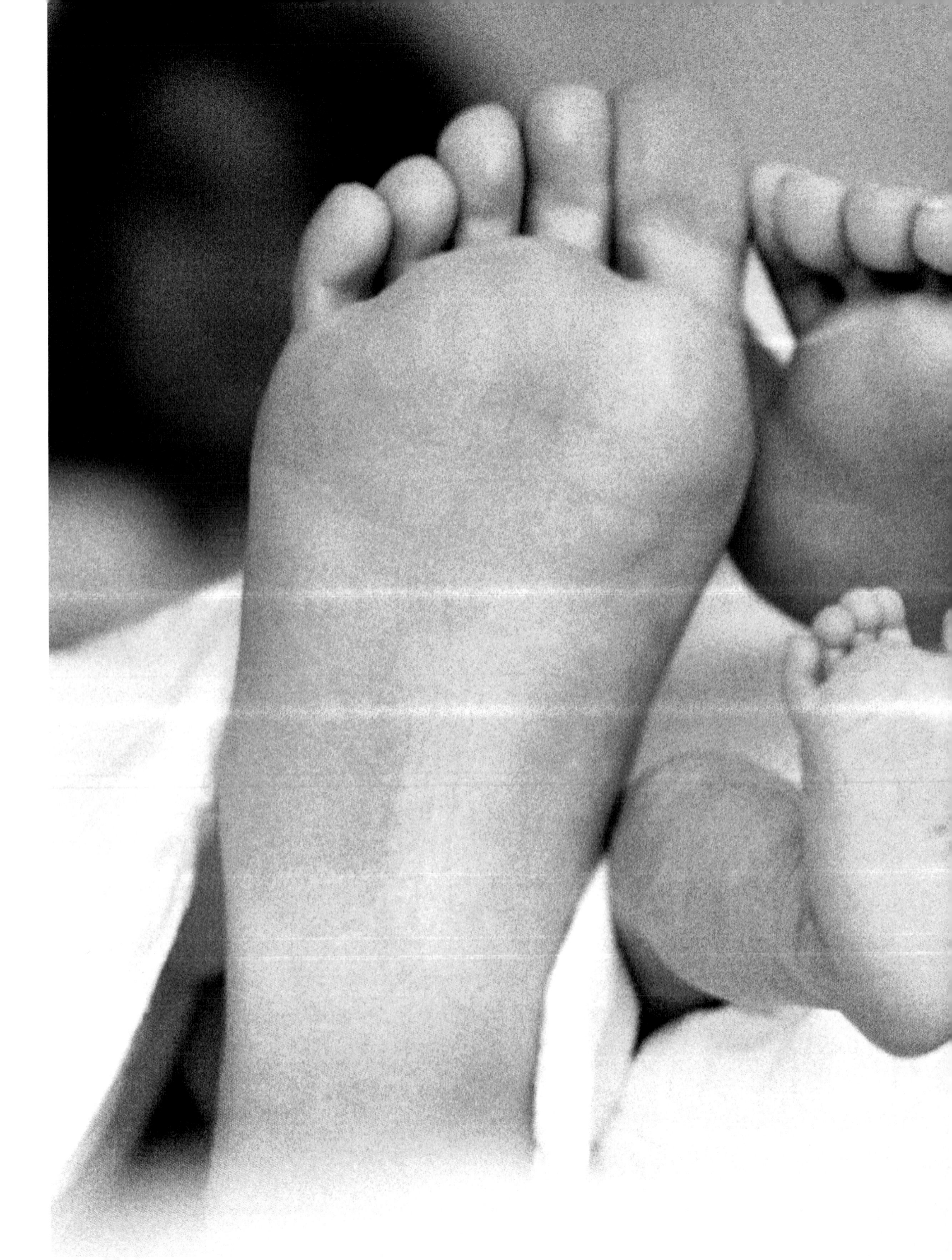

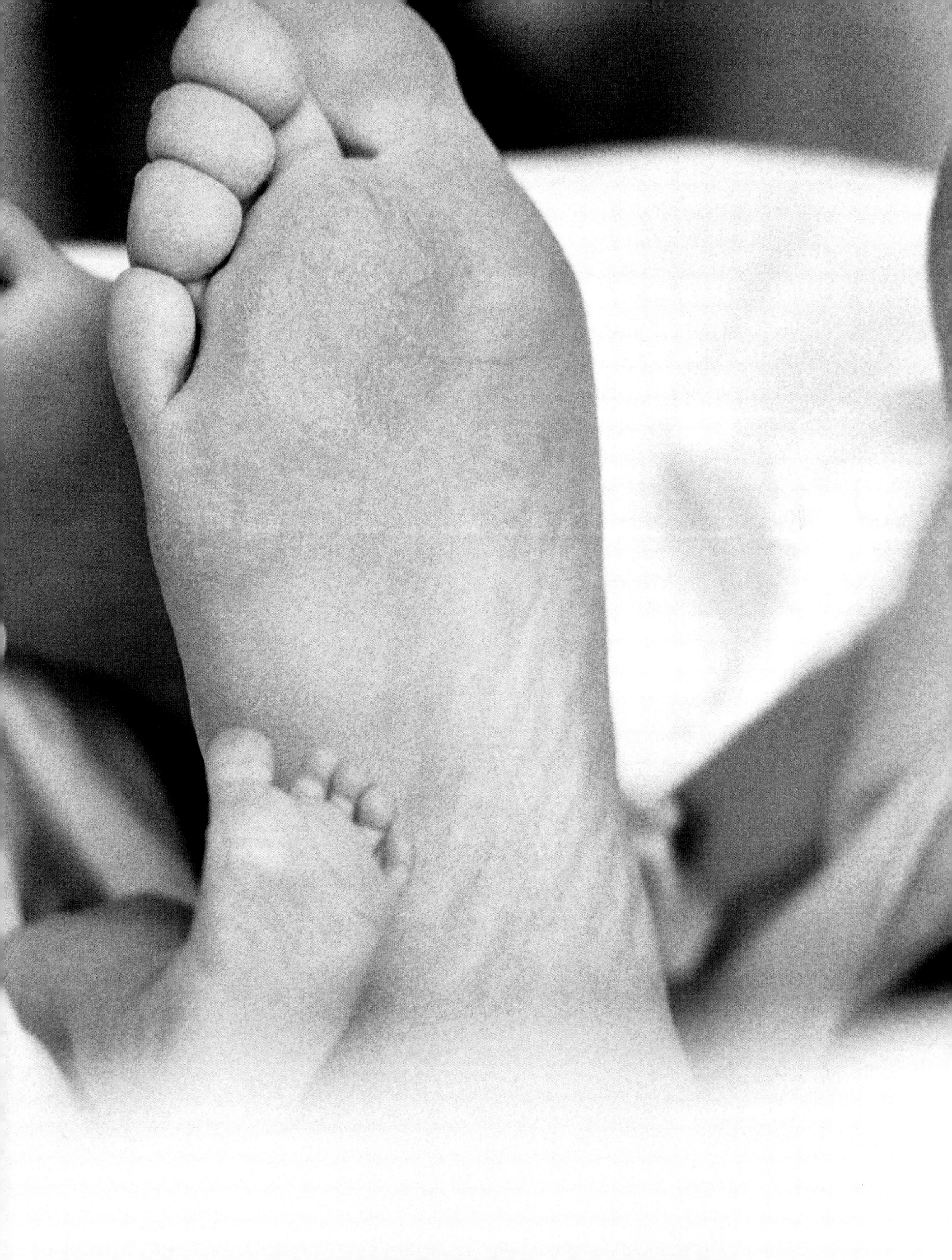

960905B p. 46

15

PAOLO
MALF

本の教文館

CHINA
TEA

1. Patrick and Cecelia
Rome 1976

2. Cindy
New York 1994

3. Hugh Grant and Elizabeth
Hurley 1997

4. Nude
St. Barthélemy 1989

5. Christy
New York 1990

6. Geisha
Tokyo 1990

7. Batoto Yeto
New York 1995

8. Billy Joel
New York 1986

9. Tatjana
Palestine Club, Egypt 1989

10. Jean-Claude Van Damme
1991

11. Joey Lauren Adams
1997

12. Cindy
New York 1988

13. Robin Williams
New York 1990

14. Warren Beatty, Annette
Bening and Their Daughter
Los Angeles 1994

15. Richard Avedon
New York 1993

16. Linda
New York 1995

17. Linda
1991

18. Paulina
New York 1987

19. Linda
1994

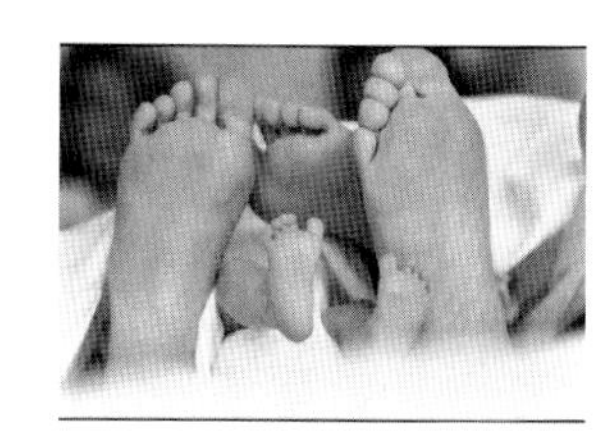

20. Billy Joel, Christie and Alexa
1986

21. Patrick Ewing
1997

22. Jean-Charles Blais
New York 1995

23. Elton John
Paris 1992

24. Johnny Depp
1986

25. Helena
New York 1992

26. Tatjana
1989

27. Kim Basinger
1985

28. Amber
Paris 1993

29. Diana
St. Barthélemy 1994

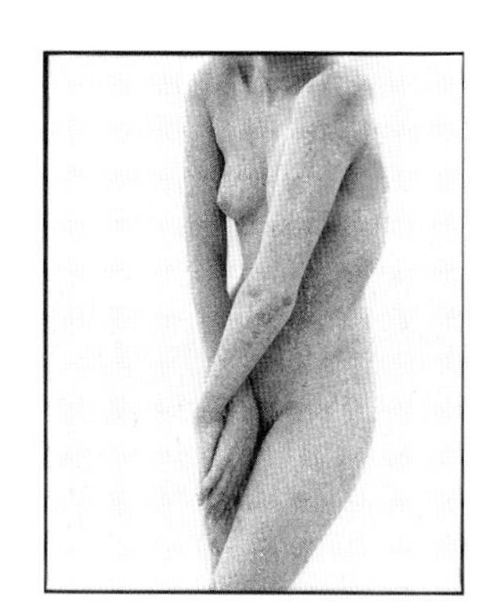

30. Nude
St. Barthélemy 1994

31. Daniel Day Lewis, Nicholas
Hytner and Winona Ryder
1996

32. Nicole Kidman
1996

33. Woman and Child
Peru 1996

34. Nadja and Julien d'Ys
1994

35. Francesco Clemente
1995

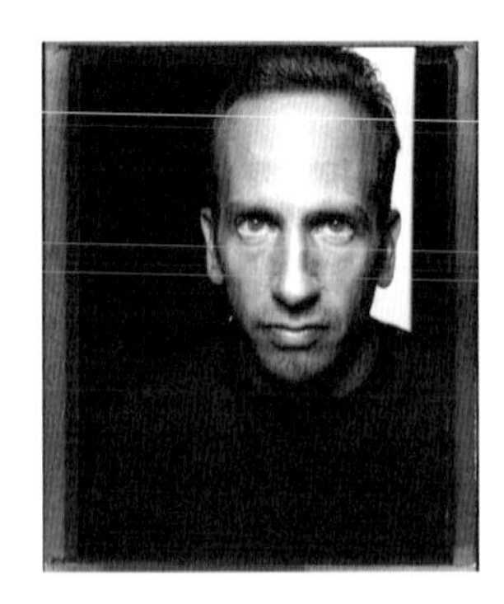

36. Kenny Scharf
1995

37. Egypt
1989

38. Julian Schnabel
1995

39. Egypt
1989

40. Priest
Tibet 1997

41. Baby Buddah
Tibet 1997

42. Sumo
1995

43. Yasmeen
New York 1993

44. Masai Warriors
Tanzania 1992

45. Charlie Korsmo from
"Dick Tracy"
Los Angeles 1989

46. Elephant
New York 1991

47. Batoto Yeto
New York 1994

48. Camel
Egypt 1989

49. Giraffes
Tanzania 1993

50. Cactus
1989

51. Giraffes
Tanzania 1993

52. Azzedine Alaïa and Yasmeen
1991

53. Cheetah
Tanzania 1993

54. Dolce and Gabbana
1997

55. Zebras
Tanzania 1993

56. Gianni Versace
Paris 1992

57. Nadja
Paris 1994

58. Georgina
1996

59. Nadja
New York 1995

60. Naomi
1991

61. Baboon
1993

62. Christy
Tokyo 1989

63. Karen
Cannes 1991

64. Kristen and Baby
1994

65. Shalom
New York 1994

66. Kate and Mannequins
1992

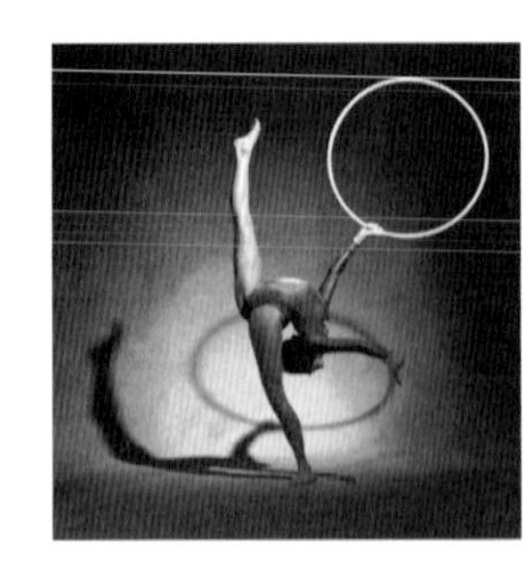

67. Dancer
1985

68. Karen Elson
St. Barthélemy 1997

69. Kristina
1996

70. Dancer
1984

71. Dancer
1984

72. Talisa Soto
1985

73. Woman on beach
1985

74. Cindy
1987

75. Christy
1987

76. Kristina
1996

77. Mathilde
1996

78. Mud Woman
1984

79. Karen Elson
St. Barthélemy 1997

80. St. Barthélemy
1997

81. Paris Collections
1997

82. Amber
1997

83. Gary Payton
1996

84. Dancer
1985

85. Nadja
St. Barthélemy 1995

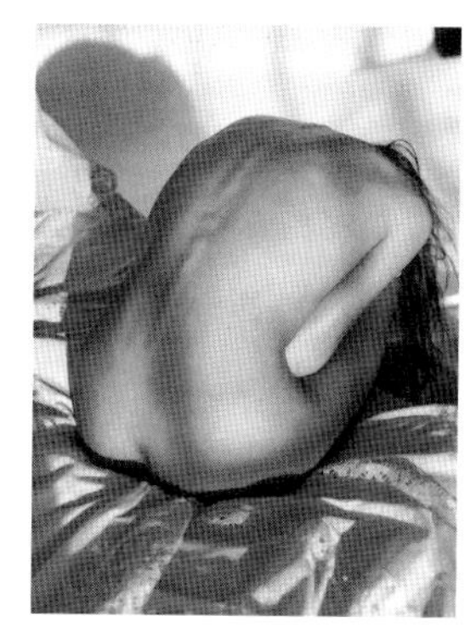

86. Rachel
1985

87. Winona Ryder
1996

88. Danielle
1997

89. Demi Moore
1997

90. Madonna
New York 1990

91. Kate Winslet
1997

92. Galliano Show
1996

93. Diana, Princess of Wales
London 1990

94. Versailles Gardens
1994

Museo de Arte Contemporáneo de Monterrey

The Museo de Arte Contemporáneo de Monterrey wishes to express its most sincere appreciation to Patrick Demarchelier, to the curator and author Martin Harrison and to Tony Shafrazi and the Tony Shafrazi Gallery for their invaluable collaboration.

MARCO also acknowledges the following individuals

Paola Gribaudo
Amanda Harrison
Ben Harrison
Wendell Maruyama
Hiroko Onoda
Tony Waddingham

This catalogue
Patrick Demarchelier: Exposing Elegance
was made possible through the generous support
of the TONY SHAFRAZI GALLERY

Permissions

Courtesy *Harper's Bazaar*, Hearst Corporation
Plates 2, 3, 11, 15, 16, 19, 25, 31, 32, 34, 43, 56, 57, 58, 59, 64, 65, 66, 68, 69, 77, 79, 80, 81, 87, 88, 89, 91, 92

Courtesy British *Vogue*, Conde Nast Publications
Plates 5, 9, 12, 17, 67, 70, 71, 73, 78, 84

Courtesy *Vogue*, Conde Nast Publications
Plate 75

Courtesy Italian *Vogue*, Conde Nast Publications
Plates 4, 6, 26, 62, 63

Courtesy Armani, Aqua Di Giò
Plate 29

Courtesy Lagerfeld, Sun Moon Stars
Plate 85

Patrick Demarchelier: Exposing Elegance
was printed in December 1997 at Pozzo Gros Monti - Fotomec in Italy. The types utilized in the composition were New Caledonia and the publication was printed on Unimatt paper. Hiroko Onoda and Jeffery J. Pavelka were responsible for overseeing the quality of the publication. Paola Gribaudo and Wendell Maruyama were in charge of supervising the printing. The print run was 2,500 copies.